Competitive Speech

Instruction and Prompts for the 2020-2021 Competitive Speech Season

Copyright © 2020 by Monument Publishing
Published by Monument Publishing
First printing, December 2020

ISBN# 979-8-582016-08-3

TABLE OF CONTENTS

INTRODUCTION TO COMPETITIVE SPEECH

By Chris Jeub

Academic speech is a vast and varied world. There are so many different events across leagues that it is difficult to keep track of the opportunities that you can take. That's what Monument is for, to bring order to the confusion and make it simple to figure out what's best for you. This preseason document introduces you to the most exciting world of competitive speech.

- Simple Explanation of Competitive Speech
- The Reasons for Speech
- Categories of Competitive Speech
- Leagues and Events for Season 21
- Resources for Members
- Final Note

Simple Explanation of Competitive Speech

Tournaments invite students to compete in selected speech events, sometimes called "Individual Events." In their schools and homes, students prepare to compete in one or more events. There are dozens of events varying from league to league, so Monument groups all events into three categories: limited-prep, platform and interp. All speeches at a tournament are judged and students are ranked and given points for their work.

The Reasons for Speech

Speech is an incredible asset to anyone with the desire to improve as a communicator. This should be everyone! There are few skills that are not universally accepted as essential that are not found in speech. Consider these five skills you will be learning:

- Confidence. They say speaking is the most frightening task, more frightening than even death! You will build confidence in doing this most daring activity.
- Brevity. You will learn how to share your thoughts in concise, easy-to-understand fashion that will be received by the listener.
- Coordination. Many speeches are timed and choreographed. Since you will deliver the speech several times, you will develop a coordination in your presentations

that will be impressive.

- Cooperation. Many speeches involve two speakers, but even so, competitive speakers learn to work in the a club and compete with other students in the same room.
- Presentation. All adults go through life having to present in front of an audience. Competitive speakers get plenty of practice in the arena of competition.

These are just a few important life skills learned in competitive speech. I have been coaching speech for decades, and all of my students become better people from competition. In fact, many of my students have had speech impediments and learning disabilities — stutterers, dyslexia, extreme shyness, etc. — and they all find events where they thrive in. Some of them even go on to championship level.

Some tend to think that speech is for those who enjoy it. Absolutely not true. Are you shy or prone to nervousness? Do a memorized interp. Are you an introvert? Write an oratory and bring out your deep thoughts.

Speech is the best extracurricular activity you can join.

That's right. The best. I used to think the written word was the best – still very important, which is why I got an English teaching degree in the first place. My first teaching job in 1995 threw me into forensics (a fancy word for all things "speech and debate"). I found that forensics had it all! Critical thinking, public speaking, persuasion, rhetoric – the list of skills mastered by the debate student was long. Those five years of coaching in the upper Midwest taught me how to teach speech and debate activities, and the next decade launched me into publishing curriculum. I've literally made speech and debate my life. Why? Because...

I believe students who master speech will master life and become the leaders our world needs.

Speech changed my entire pedagogical outlook. And you know what? I believe it should change yours, too. Whether you're a student, teacher, parent or administrator, I want you to consider:

- Students, chase after the first-place prizes during your competitive years.
- Teachers, award your best students and volunteer at every tournament.
- Parents, be your kid's #1 fan and #1 coach and #1 teacher.
- Administrators, make sure academic speech is valued just as high (if not, higher!) than other sports.

None of the above? You can participate as a judge at tournaments, volunteer to help, and ask clubs to be a part of the training. Young people are eager to perform speeches for laypeople who believe in the youth. That could be you!

I wholeheartedly believe in Monument's unique offerings for speech events. Let's get started.

Categories of Speech Events

Tournaments offer a number of events, and they usually are not organized very well when you see them. Besides, there are several different events and leagues often change things up from year to year. However, Monument Members are quickly able to assess an event by understanding the structure of the three categories. We'll get more specific as to what the big leagues offer, but for now, let's explore the three categories of speeches.

Limited-Prep

First, limited-prep events are impromptu speeches that are given from a prompt the competitors receive at the tournament.

The name "limited-prep" does not say it all in this category. There is a fair amount of preparation required as students get ready for the limited-prep event. But the preparation is more practice than it is academic preparedness. That's the part of it that's referenced by "limited-preparation." There are several individual events, two of which we develop source content: extemporaneous and apologetics.

All students are given the equivalent topics for their speaking time. For example, in an extemp round, all students will be given, say, economic questions. The point is for the judges to rate the students fairly in how they present the material. Here is a summary of the criteria judges use in ranking a limited-prep event:

1. Content. Sure, students are given the topic or question, but how they stick to the topic is just as important. Basic development of thesis, examples and illustrations reflect on how good a rhetorical speaker they are.
2. Organization. Basic understanding of the structure of a speech (introduction, body, conclusion) is ranked here.
3. Rhetoric. How succinct are the words of the speech? Does the speech have a fair balance of ethos, pathos and logos?

4. Delivery. How good a speaker is the student? The list on one league's impromptu ballot lists energy, vocal clarity, eye contact, authentic style and natural movement.
5. Overall Impression. All the limited-prep ballots ask for the judge's bottom line impression of the speaker's speech.

Each league has their own layout for limited-preparation events, but the idea is the same: train students to be great impromptu speakers. These events can vary greatly from league to league, so I won't address their differences till I talk about the leagues. For now, realize that limited-preparation is an awesome event for impromptu speakers who want to hone their impromptu skills.

Platform

Second, platform events are oratory speeches written by the students and prepared (usually memorized) for the tournament.

Young people naturally desire to express themselves, and a major focus of education should include the opportunity for self-expression within clearly defined guidelines. When a student writes an original speech and delivers it, she is taking a platform, hence the name of this type of event. There are several platform categories. Each league has their unique rules and guidelines for proper platform speaking.

Judges rank students on the same criterion as a limited-prep speaker: content, organization, rhetoric, delivery and overall impression. A typical platform speech will have many of the same characteristics as a limited-prep speech, but all platforms are prepared speeches ahead of the tournament. In other words, students will write and practice their speech ahead of time. Few of the events may allow some sort of script to be used, but most platforms are expected to be memorized and delivered at the tournament. Platform speeches are usually 10 minutes long and students are ranked among a room full of other platform speakers.

Interp

Third, interpretive (or "interp") events are literary pieces cut into a specific timeframe to present the piece of literature.

Students naturally fall in love with stories – fiction, biographies, plays – and will desire to share those stories with others. With interpretation, they have the opportunity to do so. And while they're at it, students will develop their own understanding of the literature and, more significantly, develop skills to communicate the worth of the literature.

There are several types of interpretative speeches, and all the leagues have created their unique presentation formats. I'll get to the differences in the next section, but first let me highlight the principles of all literary interpretation speeches.

Students are tasked with creating scripts or manuscripts from published literature (the only exception being Open or Original Interp where students can use original or unpublished works of literature). Students are not allowed to use one script for more than one year, and a script can only be entered in one event per tournament. Scripts have original word limitations and editing standards, and students need to keep a close eye on the event rules to make sure they are within the guidelines.

- Students are required to submit their scripts to the tournament. The leagues have individual guidelines for script submission or "Manuscript Verification Requirements." Competitors are expected to have their scripts memorized, and judges are instructed to penalize competitors if a physical script is used in the round.
- All the literary interpretation speeches are capped at 10 minutes long, no minimum. Judges are sometimes given flexibility to that maximum time in case audience participation (like laughter) drags the speech past the limit. Sometimes penalties are given for going over the time limit, but most often it is something for judges to consider on their ballots. The best competitors aim for the 10-minute mark.
- Students are tasked with cutting pieces of literature. Cutting requires reading through, then utilizing the cut-and-past tool in a word-processing program to excise parts of the literature to make it suitable for presentation. This should be done without disrespecting the content of the original piece. However, creative interpretation of a well-known piece sometimes is the most respectful interpretation you can do.
- Students are also tasked with blocking their piece. Blocking is the interper's method of acting out the piece. The interper often jumps between narration and character, and perhaps among several characters, too. The rules forbid competitors from using props, and only the speaker's feet are allowed to touch the floor, so the physical challenge of interpers are great (and impressive!). Interpers become masters of the space in the competitive room.

Few of the competitive events are as impressive as the literary interpretive events. Students come alive in front of the judges. If you've never seen one of these events, visit

YouTube and do a search for literary interpretations. Some of the recordings will certainly entertain you, and you'll simultaneously get an idea of how to do literary interpretation for competition.

Leagues and Events for Season 21

There are a lot of great leagues and organizations that share the vision of Monument: We train young people in competitive speech. Monument focuses on three leagues, but many leagues will find overlap in our releases. Besides, we don't focus on all the events of every league. There are very creative modifications and wildcard events that don't require ample source material from my Monument authors.

For this preseason document, I'll list the speech events in each league that we focus on in our memberships: NCFCA, NSDA and Stoa. If you are in a different league or organization, you will find many overlaps and similarities. Whatever community you find yourself in, seek out their website and competitive rules for each event. This will help you find the events that are most suited for your educational development.

NCFCA

The following speech categories and descriptions can be found at https://www.ncfca.org/speech/. Videos accompany these on their website.

Limited-prep:

1. Apologetics. Apologetics is a limited preparation event in which the speaker is given four minutes to prepare a six-minute speech on a topic related to articulating his or her Christian faith.
2. Extemporaneous Speaking. Extemporaneous is a limited preparation event in which the speaker is given 20 minutes to prepare a seven-minute speech on a current event topic.
3. Impromptu Speaking. Impromptu is a limited preparation speech in which the speaker is given two minutes to prepare a five-minute speech on a randomly drawn topic.

Platforms:

1. Digital Presentation. According to its website, "Digital Presentation is an original platform speech that informs or persuades and is accompanied by digital visual

aids."

2. Informative Speaking. An Informative speech is an original platform speech on any topic the speaker chooses. The primary goals of the speech are to inform, instruct, and/or inspire.

3. Persuasive Speaking. A Persuasive speech is an original platform speech that attempts to persuade the audience to adopt a particular point of view or course of action.

Interps:

1. Biblical Thematic. Note that this name has changed this season from "Presentation" to "Thematic." According to the website, "Biblical Thematic is an interpretation speech in which the speaker analyzes three or more literature selections, including at least one Scripture selection, and develops a unique, original performance using a visual aid."

2. Duo. A Duo Interpretation creatively explores and develops the intellectual, emotional, and artistic embodiment of a single selection of literature for dual performance.

3. Humorous Interpretation. According to its website, "Humorous is an interpretation speech in which the speaker explores a published literature selection and develops a unique, original, and humorous performance."

4. Open. An Open Interpretation creatively explores and develops the intellectual, emotional, and artistic embodiment of a single selection of literature for performance. This may include a piece authored by the student.

NSDA

The following speech categories and descriptions can be found at https://www.speechanddebate.org/competition-events/. Videos accompany these on their website.

Limited-prep:

1. Commentary. Students are presented with prompts related to societal, political, historic or popular culture and, in 20 minutes, prepare a five-minute speech responding to the prompt. Students may consult articles and evidence they gather prior to the contest, but may not use the Internet during preparation. The speech is delivered from memory and no notes are allowed.

2. Impromptu (Middle School). Impromptu is a public speaking event where

students have seven minutes to select a topic, brainstorm their ideas, outline and deliver a speech. The speech is given without notes and uses an introduction, body, and conclusion. The speech can be light-hearted or serious. It can be based upon prompts that range from nursery rhymes, current events, celebrities, organizations, and more.

3. International Extemporaneous Speaking. Students are presented with a choice of three questions related to international current events and, in 30 minutes, prepare a seven-minute speech answering the selected question. Students may consult articles and evidence they gather prior to the contest, but may not use the Internet during preparation. Topics range from country-specific issues to regional concerns to foreign policy. The speech is delivered from memory.

4. Mixed Extemporaneous Speaking (Middle School). Middle School Extemp combines international and domestic issues (as opposed to two separate events like high school). Students are presented with a choice of three questions related to national and international current events. The student has 30 minutes to prepare a seven-minute speech answering the selected question. Students may consult articles and evidence they gather prior to the contest, but may not use the Internet during preparation.

5. Poetry (Middle School). Using a selection or selections of literature, students provide an oral interpretation of poetry. Poetry is characterized by writing that conveys ideas, experiences, and emotions through language and expression. Students may choose traditional poetry, often characterized by rhyme or rhythm, or nontraditional poetry, which often has a rhythmic flow but is not necessarily structured by formal meter (meter is a beat, pattern, or structure, such as iambic pentameter). Students may not use prose, nor drama (plays) in this category. This event is seven minutes, including an introduction.

6. United States Extemporaneous Speaking. Students are presented with a choice of three questions related to current events in the United States and, in 30 minutes, prepare a seven-minute speech answering the selected question. Students may consult articles and evidence they gather prior to the contest, but may not use the Internet during preparation. Topics range from political matters to economic concerns to U.S. foreign policy. The speech is delivered from memory.

Platforms:

1. Declamation (Middle School). Students bring history to life- literally- by delivering a speech that has been delivered by someone else. From the historical greats to contemporary public orations, students have 10 minutes to perform a memorized

speech with an introduction. Topics can vary widely based on the interest of the student. The goal of Declamation is for the student to perform another speaker's message in their own voice.

2. Expository. Crafting an original speech, Expository students should describe, clarify, illustrate, or define an object, idea, concept, or process. The speech includes research and is aimed at informing the audience; the goal is to educate, not to advocate. No visual aids are permitted.[1] The time limit is five minutes. The speech is delivered from memory.

3. Informative Speaking. Students author and deliver a ten-minute speech on a topic of their choosing. Competitors create the speech to educate the audience on a particular topic. All topics must be informative in nature; the goal is to educate, not to advocate. Visual aids are permitted, but not required. The speech is delivered from memory.

4. Original Oratory. Students deliver a self-written, ten-minute speech on a topic of their choosing. Limited in their ability to quote words directly, competitors craft an argument using evidence, logic, and emotional appeals. Topics range widely, and can be informative or persuasive in nature. The speech is delivered from memory.

Interps:

1. Dramatic Interpretation. Using a play, short story, or other published work, students perform a selection of one or more portions of a piece up to ten minutes in length. With a spotlight on character development and depth, this event focuses on the student's ability to convey emotion through the use of a dramatic text. Competitors may portray one or multiple characters. No props or costumes may be used. Performances can also include an introduction written by the student to contextualize the performance, and state the title and the author.

2. Duo Interpretation. Two competitors team up to deliver a ten-minute performance of a published play or story. Using off-stage focus, competitors convey emotion and environment through a variety of performance techniques focusing on the relationships and interactions between the characters. No props or costumes are used. Performances can also include an introduction written by the students to contextualize the performance and state the title and the author.

3. Humorous Interpretation. Using a play, short story, or other published work, students perform a selection of one or more portions of a piece up to ten minutes

---

[1] Note that this is radically different than how NCFCA or Stoa interpret "expository." These leagues allow visual aids in their expository speeches.

in length. Humorous Interpretation is designed to test a student's comedic skills through script analysis, delivery, timing, and character development. Competitors may portray one or multiple characters. No props or costumes may be used. Performances can also include an introduction written by the student to contextualize the performance and state the title and the author.

4. Program Oral Interpretation. Using selections from Prose, Poetry and Drama students create a ten minute performance around a central theme. Program Oral Interpretation is designed to test a student's ability to intersplice multiple types of literature into a single, cohesive performance. A manuscript is required and may be used as a prop within the performance if the performer maintains control of the manuscript at all times. Performances can also include an introduction written by the student to contextualize the performance and state the title and the author of each selection.

5. Prose (Middle School). Using a short story, parts of a novel, or other published work of prose, students provide an oral interpretation of a selection of materials. Typically a single piece of literature, prose can be drawn from works of fiction or non-fiction. Prose corresponds to common speech patterns and may combine elements of narration and dialogue. Students may not use poetry, or drama (plays), in this category. This event is seven minutes, including an introduction.

6. Storytelling (Middle School). Students select a published story that meets a designated theme. Themes range widely and may include mysteries, heroism, or fairy tales. Students select a story that would be appropriate for young children and tell the story as if presenting to that audience. This event is five minutes. Students may use a chair. Manuscripts are not permitted.

Stoa

The following speech categories and descriptions can be found at http://stoausa.org/speech-events/.

Limited-prep:

1. Apologetics. In Apologetics, the competitor is given four (4) minutes to prepare a persuasive and reasoned speech that defends a tenet of the Christian faith and explains why that principle matters.

2. Extemporaneous. In Extemporaneous speaking, the competitor answers a given question based on recent events in the news. The competitor researches national and international current events and may create reference files of newsworthy

information. Extemporaneous speech should be regarded as a demonstration of personal knowledge on the topic, as well as an original synthesis of numerous sources.

3. Mars Hill. Also referred to as "Mars Hill Impromptu," the competitor in Mars Hill uses books, movies, and other genre to discuss the appeal and impact of the theme(s) within the topic, holding them up in light of Christian truth found in the Bible. This event is intended for competitors 14 and older or with the consent of the parents due to mature themes in some topics.

Platforms:

1. Expository Speaking. An Expository is a prepared speech written by the competitor which explains and illustrates a topic through both words and visuals (e.g. illustrated boards, physical props, digital and electronic presentations, or any combination).
2. Original Oratory. An Original Oratory is a prepared speech, written by the competitor, on a topic of the competitor's choice. The purpose of this informative speech is to explain, describe, or expose the topic.
3. Persuasive. A persuasive speech is a prepared speech, written by the competitor, which advocates a specific position or course of action.
4. Oratory Analysis. An Oratory Analysis is a prepared presentation of a historical or contemporary speech which includes an analysis of the content and the cultural impact of that speech, demonstrating an understanding of the context, the speaker, and the rhetorical elements that made it great. Note: This is a wildcard event that will expire after Season 21.

Interps:

1. Duo Interpretation. In Duo Interpretation, two competitors create an original rendition of a story from one or more selection(s) of literature which captivates and moves the audience.
2. Humorous Interpretation. In Humorous Interpretation, the competitors tell relatable stories using humor as a device to connect with the audience from a single published work. Stand-up comedy, or telling a series of jokes without a corresponding plot, is not Humorous Interpretation.
3. Open Interpretation. In Open Interpretation selections may be in the whole range from dramatic to humorous genres, including narrative storytelling, single voice monologues, thematic compilations, or self-written pieces.
4. Dramatic Interpretation. In Dramatic Interpretation the competitor, using a play,

short story, or other published work, performs a selection with a spotlight on character development and depth which captivates and moves the audience.

Monument Member Resources

Monument Writers consist of championship speakers and their coaches. They are a team of professionals who publish specific downloads that will help you prepare for your tournaments. We call this "source material," prepared documents that you can use to help prepare for the events that you will be competing in.

Here's how the Monument Member receives source material at MonumentMembers.com. You receive a weekly email every Monday morning at 7:00 a.m. The email lists all Monument releases for that week. For Semester 1, we are releasing three policy documents every Monday, one for each of the three leagues we cater to. Simply click through the email link, download your material, and get to work. If you missed the email, or if you want to reach back into the archive for the year, simply visit the speech category on the website. Be sure to check out the "All Downloads" page. We list all current downloads in one area to make it easy to download the source material.

We release all foundational source material by Christmas, followed by bonus material on an as-needed basis through the rest of the competitive season. Debate is the powerhouse material for competitors, but we offer two events all year long in speech:

- Extemp. Three topics are chosen from the week's headlines to cover a domestic, an international, and an economic issue. Six questions on each topic is covered.
- Impromptu. A tournament round worth of impromptu prompts will help keep the practicing member on the cutting edge of their tournament prep.

The speech categories of our website are meant to empower you for competitions. If you form the consistent habit of studying the weekly download every single week, there will be nothing stopping you from crushing it at the next tournament. You will deliver the absolute best speeches possible!

Final Note

A few years ago I ran the first tournament in Colorado for the Stoa community. It took place in November – quite early in the year, a small tournament, only the most ambitious competitors attended. Before the day started, I sent all the competitors this letter:

Dear Competitor,

I hope you're in for an AWESOME time at the tournament! My club sure is. We've been busy all week, very much looking forward to hosting the 80 competitors who will be joining together for competition tomorrow. Let me say a word about our theme, Dream Big.

I believe so much in you. You're training your mind for action, for a big purpose. Think of all those great skills you are learning in speech and debate. You'll learn and grow through every single round. The relationships you build with your fellow competitors will last a lifetime. It'll be exhausting, but you're being trained for big things.

Do me this favor: aim beyond the trophy. We spend so much time focusing on competition that people think we're out for the trophy. We want you to win, sure, but that's just the first accomplishment. We want you to apply what you learn to the great purpose life has in store for you.

Now THAT gets us excited! Don't settle for small, competitors. Dream big.

Do you catch that vision? Forgive me if I sound too sappy when I say "dream big." Perhaps it sounds sappy because dreams without the tools to achieve those dreams aren't very achievable. In fact, they seldom become reality.

But speech and debate students are being equipped with the greatest communication tools dreamers need to make their dreams come true. I honestly believe that! And your Monument Membership will help you sharpen those tools and make those dreams come true.

Are you ready for this? Probably not, but that's why we're here. If you haven't joined yet, jump in and become part of the Monument Team.

EXTEMP PROMPTS OF HEADLINE NEWS

Directions: The following is a tournament worth of extemp questions focusing on three headlines. Take time to practice answering each question, a simulation of current events at the time of this release, to keep you geared up for competition. Use the hyperlinks to read up on the latest for each topic.

Headline 1 (U.S. / Domestic): <u>George Floyd</u>

- Should the police officers fired for the death of George Floyd face more serious charges?
- Are the protests justified?
- Did Mayor DeBlasio handle the protests in New York wisely?
- How is Antifa helping or hurting the message of the Black Lives Matter movement?
- What are some of the solutions to police brutality?
- Has government leaders handled the George Floyd incident properly?

Headline 2 (World / International): <u>Covid-19</u>

- Are schools entering a crisis in numbers come fall 2020 due to Covid-19?
- What lessons were learned in the world's response to Covid-19?
- Should the World Health Organization be investigated for their response to Coronavirus?
- Is China liable for damages because of their resistance to report the Wuhan Flu?
- What countries made the best preventative policies in response to the spread of Covid-19?
- Was the Covid-19 media fair to the developing science through the pandemic?

Headline 3 (Economy / Business / Tech): <u>Social Media Censorship</u>

- Is Donald Trump's Twitter feed helpful or harmful to his agenda?
- Is Jeff Zuckerberg's defense to allow misinformation good enough?
- Should Jack Dorcey continue to fact check the president?
- Does fact checking content turn social media into a news platform that removes

liability protection?

- Is CNN a reliable source for fact checking social media posts?
- What consequences should be in place for social media censorship?

Headline 4 (U.S. / Domestic): <u>**Black Lives Matter**</u>

- Is taking a knee a show of solidarity or surrender?
- Is BLM more in line with conservative values or a liberal agenda?
- Will Donald Trump's handling of the protests be his Hurricane Katrina moment?
- Will the BLM protests move to republican or rural governmental strongholds?
- Are the BLM leaders' demands for the black community consistent with the most urgent needs of the black community?
- Will BLM have a significant platform at the Democratic Convention in August?

Headline 5 (World / International): <u>**Prince Andrew**</u>

- Is Prince Andrew a target of US prosecutors in the Jeffrey Epstein probe?
- Will the British Royal Family be able to protect Prince Andrew from testifying in US jurisdiction?
- Can current mutual assistance treaties force the hand of Queen Elizabeth to allow a statement from Prince Andrew to a British court?
- Should Virginia Roberts Giuffre testimony be believed over the Duke of York?
- Is the Department of Justice seeking publicity over accepting assistance from Prince Andrew?
- Will the Prince Andrew / Jeffrey Epstein probe lead to legislation to help put an end to human trafficking?

Headline 6 (Economy / Business / Tech): <u>**Defunding Police**</u>

- Why are some communities calling for the defunding of police forces?
- Will defunding of police departments become a democrat platform issue?
- What do mayors of LA and New York want to do with the funds saved from defunding the police?
- Have police forces become too militarized in recent years?
- Will defunding of police lead to more or less crime in poor communities?

- Will defunding of police be another flop of Joe Biden's before November's election?

Headline 7 (U.S. / Domestic): <u>Covid-19 Second Wave</u>

- Should Americans fear a second wave of coronavirus?
- Which public gatherings should be limited in number, and by how much?
- When should communities consider another shutdown of the economy to protect from a second wave of Covid-19?
- What precautions should states take to prepare for a second wave of Covid-19?
- Is fear of a second wave of coronavirus "overblown" as Mike Pence says?
- Is Beijing's second wave a concern for the Western world?

Headline 8 (World / International): <u>North Korea</u>

- Did blowing up the liaison office in Pyongyang help or hurt Kim Yo Jong position in North Korean politics?
- Why did Kim Yo Jong order the destruction of the liaison office in Pyongyang?
- Will the destruction of the liaison office harm relations between Kim Jong Un and President Trump?
- Does Kim Yo Jong stand to benefit domestically for the destruction of the Korean liaison office?
- Will the destruction of the liaison's office change Washington's view on denuclearization talks with North Korea?
- Are the Fighters for a Free North Korea leaflets doing more harm than good?

Headline 9 (Economy / Business / Tech): <u>Travel</u>

- Is it safe to travel abroad?
- What should the United States government do to help reboot the travel industry?
- What are travel industries doing to help customers feel safe while traveling?
- Are government rules on travel too much for the travel industry to comply?
- Who will be the successful transformers of the travel industry?
- Will the travel industry make a comeback much like other industries after Covid-19?

Headline 10 (U.S. / Domestic): <u>The Supreme Court</u>

- What do the Supreme Court's recent rulings reveal about the makeup of the court?
- Will the Supreme Court be as big of a voting issue in 2020 as it was in 2016?
- Why don't the Supreme Court's liberal judges often rule on conservative issues?
- Has the Roberts court punted more legal decision than ruled on law?
- Should the next appointed judge to the Supreme Court be more centrist than not?
- Has the legislative branch granted too much authority to the judicial branch?

Headline 11 (World / International): <u>Israel</u>

- Should Benjamin Netanyahu continue to push for annexation in Israeli settlements?
- What kind of security risks will Israel face as annexation continues?
- Would a Joe Biden president move the US ambassadorship back to Tel Aviv?
- Is it acceptable for a member of US Congress to question the US-Israel relationship?
- Does Israel have a comprehensive strategy to combatting its second wave of Covid-19?
- What unchartered territory will Netanyahu's corruption trial bring for Israel?

Headline 12 (Economy / Business / Tech): <u>Apple</u>

- What innovations were revealed at Apple's WWDC20?
- Will Tim Cook's decision to drop Intel and start building processors in house help or hurt the future of Apple's Macs?
- Is Apple strong enough to be a chip producer?
- How will creating its own computer chips help Apple's overall software strategy?
- Does Apple's 30% fee for its app store justify the EU's anti-trust lawsuit?
- Was Apple's decision to close most of its stores a political or strategic move?

IMPROMPTU PROMPTS

Directions: The following is a round's worth of impromptu prompts. Take time to use these prompts to sharpen your impromptu skills.

"Headline News"

Writer's Note: The following list of impromptu prompts could be done with any week of news headlines. I prepared this list by visiting Google News and selecting three of the top news stories that were hot-in-the-news during the week, then selected headlines from various sources. Students are not required to know the article exactly, but they should be able to create a short impromptu speech from basic knowledge of one of the three topics.

Speaker 1

- "Injustice began the moment police approached George Floyd." —Los Angeles Times

- "US warship sails through Taiwan Strait on Tiananmen anniversary" —Al Jazeera

- "Top U.S. scientists left out of White House selection of COVID-19 vaccine shortlist" —Science Magazine

Speaker 2

- "Trump tweets a letter calling protesters 'terrorists'" —Politico
- "Hong Kong: Tens of thousands defy ban to attend Tiananmen vigil" —BBC News
- "COVID-19 Can Last for Several Months" —The Atlantic

Speaker 3

- "Buffalo Police Officers Suspended After Shoving 75-Year-Old Protester" —The New York Times
- "The world failed after Tiananmen Square. We must not fail Hong Kong now" —The Washington Post
- "Hong Kong restaurant group's Covid-19 bible sweeps the world" —CNN

Speaker 4

- "Twitter removes Trump campaign tribute to George Floyd claiming copyright complaint" —The Hill
- "31 Yrs After Tiananmen Massacre, Mothers of Victims Await Answers" —VOA News
- "The first wave of Covid-19 is not over — but how might a second look?" —The Guardian

Speaker 5

- "Civil Rights Groups, Black Lives Matter Sue Trump Administration Over Protest Violence" —NPR
- "Ki Thinks Tiananmen Was Worth It" —Foreign Policy
- "Vital UN peace and security work continues amid COVID-19 challenge" —UN News

Speaker 6

- "George Floyd: African-Americans are more likely to get fatally shot" —BBC News
- "US Presses China for 'Full Public Accounting' of 1989 Tiananmen Crackdown" —Voice of America
- "Are Symptoms From COVID-19 or Seasonal Allergies?" —WebMD

"Television Cops"

Reworked from a list provided by "The 25 Most Unforgettable Cops in Television History," Fox News, accessed June 9, 2020. https://www.foxnews.com/lifestyle/the-25-most-unforgettable-cops-in-television-history

Speaker 1

- Frank Columbo: 'Columbo'
- Frank Drebin: 'Police Squad!'
- Olivia Benson: 'Law & Order: SVU'

Speaker 2

- Pete, Julie and Linc: 'The Mod Squad'

- Barney Fife: 'The Andy Griffith Show'
- Horatio Caine, 'CSI: Miami'

Speaker 3

- Hank Schrader: 'Breaking Bad'
- Andy Sipowicz: 'NYPD Blue'
- David Starsky and Kenneth Hutchinson: 'Starsky & Hutch'

Speaker 4

- Chief Wiggum: 'The Simpsons'
- Mike Stone and Steve Keller: 'The Streets of San Francisco'
- NYC's 12th Precinct Detectives: 'Barney Miller'

Speaker 5

- Lennie Briscoe: 'Law & Order'
- Carl Winslow, 'Family Matters'
- Vince Masuka: 'Dexter'

Speaker 6

- Joe Friday: 'Dragnet'
- James Crockett and Ricardo Tubbs: 'Miami Vice'
- The Hill Street Blues: 'Hill Street Blues'

"Favorites"

Speaker 1

- My favorite color
- My favorite dog breed
- My favorite vacation

Speaker 2

- My favorite animal
- My favorite president

- My favorite season

Speaker 3

- My favorite actor
- My favorite country
- My favorite feeling

Speaker 4

- My favorite place
- My favorite memory
- My favorite pet

Speaker 5

- My favorite friend
- My favorite movie
- My favorite car

Speaker 6

- My favorite hobby
- My favorite television show
- My favorite politician

"20th Century President Quotes"

Adapted from Yara Coelho, "55 Inspiring Quotes from U.S. Presidents That Will Change Your Life," Lifehack, Accessed June 22, 2020. https://www.lifehack.org/articles/productivity/55-inspiring-quotes-from-presidents-that-will-change-your-life.html

Speaker 1

- "It is hard to fail, but it is worse never to have tried to succeed." — Theodore Roosevelt
- "When our memories outweigh our dreams, it is then that we become old." — Bill Clinton

- "The hottest places in hell are reserved for those who, in times of great moral crisis, maintain their neutrality." — John F. Kennedy

Speaker 2

- "Do what you can, with what you have, where you are." — Theodore Roosevelt
- "We all do better when we work together. Our differences do matter, but our common humanity matters more." — Bill Clinton
- "It's amazing what you can accomplish if you do not care who gets the credit." — Harry S. Truman

Speaker 3

- "Be patient and calm; no one can catch a fish with anger." — Herbert Hoover
- "We all do better when we work together. Our differences do matter, but our common humanity matters more." — Bill Clinton
- "Conformity is the jailer of freedom and the enemy of growth." — John F. Kennedy

Speaker 4

- "Words without actions are the assassins of idealism." — Herbert Hoover
- "A volunteer is a person who can see what others cannot see; who can feel what most do not feel. Often, such gifted persons do not think of themselves as volunteers, but as citizens – citizens in the fullest sense: partners in civilization." — George H.W. Bush
- "Never waste a minute thinking about people you don't like." — Dwight D. Eisenhower

Speaker 5

- "The only thing we have to fear is fear itself." — Franklin D. Roosevelt
- "Live simply, love generously, care deeply, speak kindly, leave the rest to God." — Ronald Reagan
- "It's amazing what you can accomplish if you do not care who gets the credit." — Harry S. Truman

Speaker 6

- "I have opinions of my own – strong opinions – but I don't always agree with them." — George H.W. Bush

- "Remember, remember always, that all of us, and you and I especially, are descended from immigrants and revolutionists." — Franklin D. Roosevelt
- "What counts is not necessarily the size of the dog in the fight- it's the size of the fight in the dog." — Dwight D. Eisenhower

Monument Members receive prompts like these ALL YEAR LONG in ALL leagues. Never be caught without a response in a speech round: MonumentMembers.com.

Champion Speakers Are Always Ready!

Become a Monument Member and receive weekly cases, briefs, and downloads that will guide you to successful tournament competition!

"Monument has taken my coaching from 0 to 60 in a flash! Our entire club has benefited greatly from all the current season materials immensely… We're getting loads of value from Monument and recommend them highly!" —Joseph G., WA

"Monument is a critical tool to the success and development of our club. The tools and resources available are unmatched." —Mike D., Washington

"You make teaching debate a thousand times easier. I would not coach a kid who didn't have Monument PERIOD. I don't have time to reinvent the wheel every season!! Thank you." —Janine W., Missouri

"I'm always impressed with the quality of Monument's content. This is always my first stop for speech and debate prep, both for my students and to better prepare myself for teaching." —Jennifer M., Indiana

Just Minutes Of Preparation Every Week — Save Endless Hours Web Searching and Screen Time…Guaranteed!

MonumentMembers.com/join

www.ingramcontent.com/pod-product-compliance
Lightning Source LLC
Chambersburg PA
CBHW081406160726
48000CB00010B/3491